The Turks and Caicos Islands

Lands of Discovery

Third Edition

Amelia Smithers
Revised and updated by Anthony Taylor

MACMILLAN
CARIBBEAN

Macmillan Education
Between Towns Road, Oxford OX4 3PP
A division of Macmillan Publishers Limited
Companies and representatives throughout the world

www.macmillan-caribbean.com

ISBN 0 333 92961 6

First published 1990
Reprinted 1991
Second edition 1995
Third edition 2003

Typeset by CjB Editorial Plus
Cover design by Gary Fielder, AC Design
Cover photographs: (front) West Sand Spit is located on the edge of
the Caicos Bank, southeast of Providenciales, and is a superb venue
for diving. (Back) Hobie Cat races are a highlight of the annual Fool's
Regatta which usually takes place in May or June. (Both photographs
by Kathleen McNary Wood)

The authors and publishers would like to thank the following
for permission to reproduce their material:
Charlene Kozy, the late Herbert E. Sadler, Paul Albury,
Michael Craton and the Public Records Office, Kew, England.

The authors and publishers would like to thank the following
for permission to reproduce their photographs:
Stephen Frink/Waterhouse, G. W. Lennox, The Mansell Collection,
Doug Perrine, Brian Riggs, Phil Shearer, Anthony Taylor, Turks and
Caicos Islands Tourist Board, Turks and Caicos National Museum,
Maggie Walker, Alan Wizemann, Kathleen McNary Wood.

Printed and bound in Malaysia

2007 2006 2005 2004 2003
10 9 8 7 6 5 4 3 2 1

| Contents |

Barrelling salt on Grand Turk (TURKS AND CAICOS NATIONAL MUSEUM)

| Preface |

The Turks and Caicos Islands have experienced rapid growth since the second edition of this book was published over six years ago. Thanks to increased flights to the Islands and a burgeoning travel industry, the Islands are fast becoming a much sought after destination for a variety of travellers and holiday-makers. This has led to a wide choice of hotels and resorts and rapidly improving facilities.

It is this change in the Islands that has necessitated the third revision of this excellent book. The first and second editions were both written by the book's author, Amelia Smithers, and where possible I have left her original work untouched. The chapters on Providenciales and Grand Turk have been extensively revised to reflect the shift of influence between the two islands as a result of the rapid development of Providenciales.

Numerous people have helped me in the preparation of this third edition, offering their time, knowledge and skill. I am extremely grateful for their help, as without it this edition would not have been done.

Anthony Taylor

August 2001

Preface to the Second Edition

The Turks and Caicos Islands have experienced many changes since the first edition of this guide was published more than four years ago. The Islands are gradually becoming better known as a travel destination, and facilities have greatly improved.

Many people have helped in the preparation of this second edition and I should particularly like to thank Mr Jude Bernard and Mr Stanley Astwood of the Turks and Caicos Tourist Board for their assistance and helpful suggestions, the Director of the JoJo Project, Dean Bernell, Island Photo of Providenciales and Countess Helen Czernin.

The chapter on the history of the Islands is largely based on research conducted by the late H. E. 'Bertie' Sadler whose death in 1992 greatly saddened all who knew him. I am once more grateful to Mr Josiah Marvel for his erudite assistance as regards the early history of the Islands and to Dr Charlene Kozy of the University of Tennessee who allowed me to quote passages from her paper on the history of the Loyalist settlers. As in the previous edition, my thanks also go to Dr George Proctor of the Department of Natural Resources, Puerto Rico, whose knowledge of the flora of the Islands was invaluable in preparing the natural history chapter. I am also appreciative of the help and assistance given by Karen Collins and Artistic Licence Ltd. of Grand Turk.

Finally, my thanks go to the Director of Macmillan Caribbean, Bill Lennox, whose enthusiasm and love of the Caribbean islands led to the publication of this book.

Amelia Smithers
July 1994

JoJo the dolphin breaching a wave off Providenciales *(opposite)* (DOUG PERRINE)

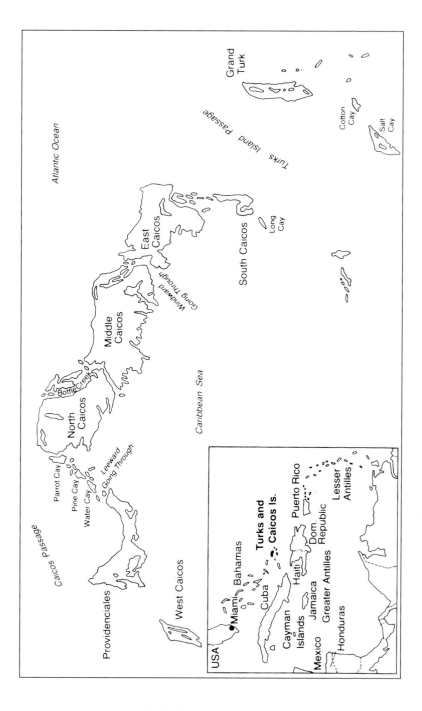

The Turks and Caicos Islands

| 1 |
Where on Earth are the Turks and Caicos Islands?

'Where on Earth are the Turks and Caicos Islands?' was a question that used to appear on advertisements put out by the Islands' Tourist Board some years ago. 'Beyond the Bahamas - closer than the Caribbean' was the reply. In fact this archipelago of low-lying islands, six of which are inhabited, lies a short 575 miles southeast of Miami, and just north of Haiti and the Dominican Republic. They cover a total of some 150 square miles.

The Tourist Board has long since changed its slogan as the Islands have opened up to tourism but the Turks and Caicos are still one of the least known Caribbean destinations – although technically they are in the Atlantic. The name of the country has perhaps contributed to its unfamiliarity. Two explanations have been offered for the derivation of the name 'Turks'; one is that it refers to the time when the area was much favoured by pirates from the Mediterranean who were commonly known as 'Turks'; the other is that the red dome (cephalium) surrounding the Islands' native Turk's cap cactus (*Melocactus intortus*) reminded early settlers of a Turkish fez. Caicos is believed to be derived from the Spanish 'cayos' meaning rocky islands of cays.

Visitors to the Islands, arriving by plane for the first time, are struck by the transparency of the sparkling turquoise waters, making the Tourist Board's new slogan 'Beautiful by Nature' more apt. From the air, the land looks flat and covered with scrubby vegetation. This uniformity is deceptive however, and once on the ground the different physical characteristics of each Island become more apparent.

The rainfall in the Caicos Islands is much higher than that of the Turks Islands and on North Caicos tropical fruit trees, such as bananas and mangoes, are common. However, on Grand Turk only the most drought tolerant plants, such as the scarlet cordia (*Cordia sebestena*) with its bright orange blooms and the yellow elder (*Tecoma stans*) a native shrub with clusters of yellow flowers, survive without special care.

The differences between the Islands are not only physical: whilst Providenciales, commonly shortened to Provo, continues to grow as a cosmopolitan resort, Grand Turk, with its historic buildings, remains an old-fashioned tightly knit town where everyone knows (and is often related to) everyone else.

While the Turks and Caicos Islands are a British Overseas Territory with a Governor appointed by Britain, North America exerts more direct influence. The US dollar is the official currency and almost all food and other items are flown or shipped in from Florida. Indeed most residents are more familiar with Miami, New York and Freeport,

Canons stand guard in front of the Legislative Council building (ALAN WIZEMANN)

than they are with London or Manchester. This is largely because, unlike other British and former British territories in the region, there has been virtually no emigration to Britain from the Turks and Caicos, and partly because of the influence of US television which is received via satellite. Islanders looking for better prospects away from their own shores, have tended to move to the US, Canada and the Bahamas. In recent years, many young people who were raised and educated in the Bahamas, have returned to take advantage of the new opportunities offered by the burgeoning economy on Providenciales.

The waters around the cays off Providenciales are sparkling and clear

Other appearances are deceptive as well; whilst Grand Turk's oldie-worldy appearance may recall a bygone era, behind many of its historic buildings state-of-the-art satellite communications and computers keep the Islands' lawyers, bankers and accountants in constant touch with the financial centres of the world. Both the government and the private sector are committed, in fact, to maintaining the Turks and Caicos as a reputable centre for offshore finance.

Sunset over Grace Bay Beach from the Sibonne Hotel *(opposite)*
(ANTHONY TAYLOR)

| 2 |
Natural history

Visitors to the Turks and Caicos Islands are sometimes disappointed by what at first may seem like dull, scrubby vegetation. In fact, although the coral limestone of the Islands cannot rival the lush volcanic mountains of Jamaica and other islands, they do support a rich, diverse and unique plant and animal life.

The visitor who arrives in the Turks and Caicos by boat, passing mile after mile of uninhabited cays and mangrove swamps, is much more aware of the Islands' extensive landmass than the person arriving by plane on Providenciales or Grand Turk. The Turks and Caicos Islands are intriguing in that two of the islands - East and West Caicos - are totally uninhabited (the land belongs to the Crown) whilst North and Middle Caicos support only a tiny population in relation to their total landmass.

Coastal rock plant communities are crafted by the forces of wind and salt spray creating beautiful natural bonsai gardens (KATHLEEN MCNARY WOOD)

Vegetation

The plant life of the Turks and Caicos Islands has evolved over hundreds of thousands of years into a unique ecosystem adapted to the prevailing influence of the sea. The native vegetation of Providenciales, for instance, consists largely of scrubby bush interwoven with small palms, cactus, agave, yucca and other succulents, to create a year-round tapestry of colour and texture.

The Caicos Islands are, as mentioned before, far more fertile than the Turks Islands. Instead of low, dry, rocky hills covered with scrub, the visitor from Grand Turk who arrives on North Caicos finds himself surrounded by a dense growth of large trees including *Bucida bucera*, known locally as 'oak' and the mahogany tree (*Swietenia mahagoni*) which is called 'Madeira' and from which the wheels, of donkey carts used to be made. Fruit trees such as banana and mango, which could never grow on Grand Turk without artificial irrigation, grow here with such abundance and vigour that the Grand Turk gardener is left wondering why he (or she) bothers at all.

Both North and Middle Caicos have, in areas where there is considerable ground water, examples of native Caribbean pine, a beautiful tropical pine tree. In the Turks Islands, particularly on Grand Turk, opinion is divided as to whether the vegetation was originally as sparse as it is today, or whether there were once more of the small trees and shrubs, such as palmettos, found on the Caicos Islands but they were cut down by the first settlers. Evidence for the latter opinion is to be found in regulations made in Grand Turk in 1767 which, among other things, laid down penalties 'for persons cutting down palmetto – young thatch trees being so necessary to the inhabitants for their houses and for covering their salt'.

Cactus and succulents are abundant throughout the Islands. Sadly, so many Turk's cap cacti have been dug up that, apart from the ones in people's gardens, they are now only found growing wild in the most remote and inaccessible areas. Apart from the cordia and yellow elder already mentioned, ornamental trees and shrubs have been introduced, such as the flame tree (*Delonix regia*), hibiscus (*Hibiscus rosa-sinensis*) and bougainvillea (*Bougainvillea spectabilis*), creating a riot of colour in many gardens, even at the driest times of the year.

Unfortunately, in the course of developing new houses and hotels, the conservation of native vegetation is sometimes overlooked. However, three indigenous species do have interesting stories linked with them. For instance the wood of the steely, slow-growing lignum-vitae

Silver palms are a characteristic feature of the landscape of the Turks and Caicos (KATHLEEN MCNARY WOOD)

tree, the 'tree of life' (*Guaiacum officinale*), with its profusion of powder blue blooms, is so dense that it does not float in water, while the unusually named Gumbo Limbo tree is often called the 'tourist tree' as its red bark resembles the pink skin of sunburn. Beware not to confuse the Gumbo Limbo with the similar looking, but nasty, Poison Wood whose sap causes painful skin blistering and cannot be washed off as it is not water soluble. Wily locals know to use WD40 to remove the sap!

Today, some of the trees most commonly found in the Turks Islands include: *Casuarina equisetifolia*, an Australian native; the coconut (*Coconut nuciferae*); the scarlet cordia (*Cordia sebestena*); the tamarind (*Tamarindus indicus*); the guinep (*Melicoccus bijugatus*); the sapodilla (*Manilkara zapotilla*); the Canary date palm (*Phoenix canariensis*);

and, a recent introduction, the tropical neemes, a graceful tree with feathery, light green leaves which grows very fast and is drought tolerant. One of the oldest and largest neemes in the Islands is located in front of the Meridian Club on Pine Cay.

Birds and beasts

The Turks and Caicos are home to many tropical sea birds and are also the temporary home of many species of migratory birds. The flamingo, which figures on the coat of arms, is a shy bird and stays away from the main centres of population. It is an occasional visitor to Grand Turk's North Creek, and flocks of flamingoes are occasionally spotted by low-flying aircraft on uninhabited East and West Caicos.

Bird watchers will find much to keep them busy on any of the Islands. Herons are quite common and can be seen wading in Grand Turk's shallow salinas, quite undisturbed by the traffic and passers-by.

In the Caicos Islands there are many species of birds not found in the Turks Islands. When I first visited North Caicos, I heard what

An iguana stands guard on Little Water Cay (PHIL SHEARER)

sounded like a parrot, but was in fact a local crow known as 'laughing crow' which sounds just like a parrot.

The Islands' native animal population consists mostly of non-poisonous snakes and lizards. On the uninhabited cays, colonies of iguana are quite tame and they can be hand-fed.

In February, the Islands are on the migratory passage of humpback whales, as they pass through Turks Island Passage on their way to the Mouchoir Banks. Each winter, the entire Atlantic herd – some 2500 humpback whales – make the migration. Divers are occasionally treated to underwater concerts of the whales' songs. Most sightings of whales are made in February and March. Some are even lucky enough to witness every Caribbean diver's dream and encounter a female humpback whale with a newborn calf.

JoJo

Dolphins are also often seen in the waters around the Turks and Caicos Islands and one dolphin in particular, has become something of a local personality.

A manta ray glides majestically off Provo (PHIL SHEARER)

For many years, people living on Providenciales, North Caicos and Pine Cay, had knowledge of a dolphin who was particularly friendly with humans. It was only when **Club Méditerranée** opened its 'Turkoise' resort in 1984, however, that the dolphin became something of a local star. Almost every day, as guests came down to the beach, the dolphin would be there to meet them. He was given the name 'JoJo' after the Club's first 'Chef du Village' and he continues to make friends with the thousands of tourists who stay at Club Med and other beach-side hotels.

Almost everyone will have seen dolphins in captivity – where they apparently often die of depression. What is unique about JoJo is that he is a wild animal who forsakes the company of his own kind to inter-mingle with humans.

Sadly, of the few dolphins in the world that either choose, like Jo-Jo, to seek out human companionship or were captured in the wild, few survive the experience. It was for this reason that **The JoJo Dolphin Project** was set up. The project, established under the aus-pices of Prince Sadruddin Aga Khan's **Bellerive Foundation**, aims to increase the chances of survival of JoJo and other dolphins by under-standing their needs and natural behaviour.

JoJo plays alongside Big Blue's dive boat in Leeward Marina (PHIL SHEARER)

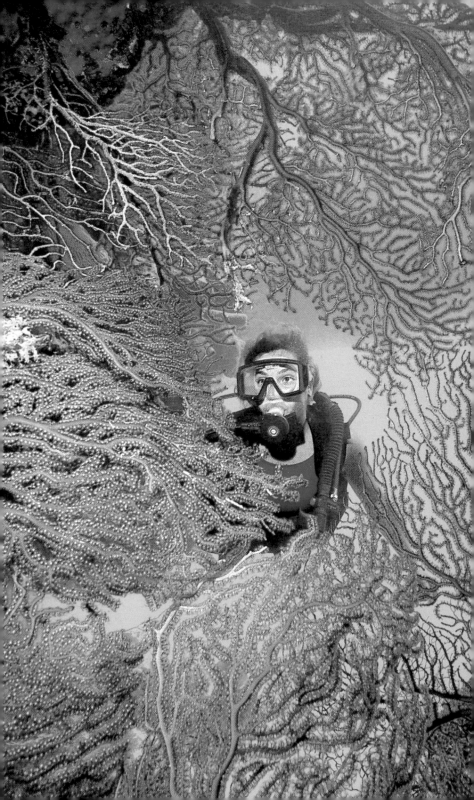

The organisation provides JoJo and other cetaceans with specialised veterinary assistance and gives visitors tips on how to handle dolphin encounters. A full-time warden, **Dean Bernell** spends time with JoJo and studies his behaviour. The advice given to visitors should they be approached by JoJo in the water, is that they should never touch him, neither should they chase him nor lie on their backs when with him.

Coral gardens

If, to the critical eye, the Turks and Caicos cannot hold a candle to other so-called tropical paradises above the water-line, the visitor who dons mask and snorkel or even better scuba, immediately enters a world of unsurpassable beauty.

To the diver who has experienced other diving locations around the world, the advantages offered by the Turks and Caicos Islands are:

- the reefs are mostly in pristine condition;
- they lie in relatively shallow water, doing away with the need for inconvenient decompression stops;
- for the most part, the sites are only short boat rides from shore.

The main diving schools, which are recognised by PADI (the US Professional Association of Diving Instructors) are located on Grand Turk and Providenciales. Several of the diving schools on Providenciales organise diving trips to West Caicos and to outlying reefs. The Island also has a recompression chamber.

Many dive sites are located on the 'Wall'. This is where the shallow seabed inside the reef plunges abruptly to some 7000 feet. From the shore, the Wall is visible as a line of colour demarcating the two depths, on one side the shallow pale turquoise waters, on the other the deep blue ocean. The effect is not much different underwater. The diver swimming over the Wall for the first time, may if she or he is susceptible to such things, experience some giddiness when peering down the wall of coral. As far as the eye can see, there extrude sponges in shades of orange and yellow, some shaped like rope, others like Victorian bath tubs, and iridescent coral encrustations between which dart schools of brightly coloured fish and the occasional larger solitary predator such as a barracuda, a manta ray or a turtle.

Underwater scene showing coral *(opposite)*
(STEPHEN FRINK)

A turtle is a common sight for snorkellers and divers (PHIL SHEARER)

Some of the Islands' diving sites are named after particular characteristics, others after landmarks on the Island that help to identify them. Thus, **Finbar's Reef** is named after local attorney and one-time magistrate Finbar Dempsey, while **Chief Minister's Reef** is named after its landmark, the former residence of a chief minister, and at the **Amphitheatre** you can sit on a clearing of pure white sand 60 feet under the surface, gazing up at the Roman-style amphitheatre of coral all around you.

Environmental awareness

The people of the Turks and Caicos are increasingly aware of their country's rich and hitherto unspoilt natural heritage. National parks have now been established to protect both designated wilderness areas on land and the Islands' spectacular coral reefs. One of these national parks, the Princess Alexandra National Park, opened by Britain's Princess Alexandra in November 1988, encompasses about half of Providenciales' northern shore, from Little Water Cay to Turtle Cove.

The imposing osprey is often seen around Turtle Cove (PHIL SHEARER)

The parks are designed to allow visitors to enjoy wilderness areas without harming their delicate ecosystems. Boating, recreational line fishing, swimming and scuba diving are allowed in the parks. Spearfishing, diving for lobster and conch, and jet-skiing are not.

In addition to the national parks, the Turks and Caicos government has also set up nature reserves, sanctuaries and historical sites totalling more than 325 square miles. Of this total amount, 210 square miles are areas designated as sensitive and ecologically essential wetlands. Other protected areas include marine replenishment areas as well as breeding grounds for turtles, seabirds and other creatures. A national environment centre, in The Bight, is under construction and is one of many initiatives to protect the country's wildlife.

| 3 |
History

The history of the Turks and Caicos can be divided into six parts:
- pre-Columbian history;
- the Columbus Landfall;
- the Bermudian settlement and the salt industry;
- the Loyalist settlement of the Caicos Islands;
- Jamaican rule;
- the Turks and Caicos since 1962.

Pre-Columbian history: the Lucayans

The earliest inhabitants of the Islands were Arawak Indians known as Lucayans. Long-time resident of Grand Turk, H E Sadler, author of *Turks Islands Landfall*, writes:

> *The aboriginal Indians of the Turks Islands are believed to have initially migrated from South America to escape the rapacious Carib tribes, who practised cannibalism in the wild Orinocco Delta.*

The Lucayans' largest settlements appear to have been on East and Middle Caicos where the caves provided sanctuary in times of hurricane. Hunraken was the Lucayan god of evil. There are 38 pre-Columbian sites on Middle Caicos. The Lucayans traded salt and dried conch with the Tainos tribe of Hispaniola to whom they were related. Excavations also unearthed a traditional Indian ballcourt where the Lucayans played a game with a ball made of natural rubber, a material then unknown to the Spaniards. Recent excavations on Grand Turk have also revealed Lucayan beads which are now on display at the Turks and Caicos National Museum on Grand Turk.

Columbus described the Lucayan Indians as living in conical thatched huts. The Chief's house was larger than the rest. According to Sadler, the Lucayans grew tobacco and rolled the leaves to make cigars, or ground them to make snuff. Gonzalo de Oviedo y Valdes, in his 1535 history of the New World, related how the Indians drew the snuff into their noses through a Y-shaped pipe which they called 'tobacco'. This

A guide shines a torch in one of Middle Caicos's extensive caves (BRIAN RIGGS)

word was soon universally used to denote the plant itself when it was introduced into Europe.

The Lucayans also cultivated sea island cotton which they used for making hammocks and mosquito nets. They carved wood and stone and wove baskets. Some of their wooden carvings and stone celts, as well as items of pottery, have been discovered in various archaeological excavations in the Caicos Islands, starting with de Booy's excavations in 1912. Sadly, most of the finds of these early digs were either taken out of the country or have gone missing.

The Columbus Landfall

On 12 October 1492 the Lucayans' peaceful existence was interrupted by the arrival of Christopher Columbus, who made his first landfall in the Americas on an island he called Guanahani.

Traditionally, it has been held that Guanahani was the present-day island of San Salvador in the Bahamas, although in 1986, *National Geographic* magazine published an article claiming that Samana Cay, also in the Bahamas, was the site of the Landfall. Another school of thought contends that the Landfall, in fact, took place on Grand Turk.

Columbus lands at 'Guanahani', believed by many to be the present-day Grand Turk, in 1492 (THE MANSELL COLLECTION)

Those who support the Grand Turk Landfall, including Sadler and another local historian, Josiah Marvel, base their arguments on the description of Guanahani given by Columbus himself. Marvel outlined his argument in an article *Columbus* in the Fall 1989 issue of *Times of the Island*s, the quarterly magazine of the Turks and Caicos.

The Grand Turk Landfall theory was first put forward by the respected nineteenth century Spanish historian Fernandez de Navarette and is gaining ground in modern academic circles. In December 1989, a Grand Turk Landfall Symposium was held in Grand Turk, attended by experts in the field including leading Spanish historians and a direct descendant of Christopher Columbus.

At any rate, when the Lucayans of Guanahani first saw the Spaniards, with their strange appearance, clothes, boats and weapons, they mistook them for superior beings sent from Heaven and offered them food and drink.

As Paul Albury wrote in his book *The Story of the Bahamas*:

This delusion, understandable under the circumstances, was probably the most tragic mistake those gentle people ever made.

Although, in his diary, Columbus recorded his admiration for the Indians' physique and their cheerful dispositions, he was soon calculating how their timidity could be exploited and wrote home:

When your Highness so command, they can all be carried off to Castille or held captive in the Island itself, since with fifty men they would all be kept in subjection and forced to do what ever may be wished.

The Lucayans did not survive their encounter with the Spaniards. Many were carried off into captivity to be used as slaves in Hispaniola or as pearl divers off the coast of Venezuela. Pearl fisheries were then lucrative sources of wealth in the Indies, but Indian divers were needed to collect them. The Spaniards organised successive slave raids into the Bahamas to capture the men they needed. Bishop Las Casas wrote:

The tyranny which the Spanish exercise against the Indians in the gathering or fishing for pearls is one of the most cruel and condemnable things that could ever be on earth. There is no more infernal nor insane life in this century with which it could be compared ... They put them into the sea in three, four or five fathoms depth, from morning until sundown; they are always underwater, swimming without being able to catch their breath, tearing off the oysters in which the pearls grow. They come back to the surface for air with a small net filled with them, when a cruel Spaniard waits in a canoe or small boat, and if they take long in resting, he gives them blows and shoves them under the water by the hair to dive again. Their meals are fish, oysters, cassava and some corn, with which they are never filled to excess. The bed they give them at night is to secure them in stocks in the ground, so they will not escape. Many times they dive into the sea and never return to the surface, because the sharks, which can devour an entire man, kill and eat them.

By 1513, it is estimated that there was not a single Lucayan left in the Turks and Caicos Islands or the surrounding islands now forming part of the Bahamas. When Ponce de Leon stopped at Grand Turk in 1512, the Spanish historian Herrera recorded that he could only find one old Indian left on the Island to assist him in his search for 'Bimini', the legendary fountain of youth. Some maps of the time show Grand Turk as 'Del Viejo', meaning the island of the Old Man.

After the abduction of its Indian population, the Turks and Caicos were uninhabited. They continued to be a popular port of call for early Spanish mariners, who stopped for precious salt on the way home to Spain. Many a Spanish galleon came to grief on the treacherous reefs surrounding the Islands, taking artifacts and weaponry with them to the sea floor.

A few years ago, one of these ships, known as the Molasses Reef Wreck, was raised in waters off the Turks and Caicos Islands and taken to an institute of nautical archaeology in Texas, where centuries of encrustation was removed. The small Spanish ship, which was found to be heavily armed, was carrying Lucayan pottery which means that it must have sunk before the extermination of the Lucayans c1513. The ship has not yet been identified but it has been determined that it is not Columbus' caravel, the *Pinta*, which has never been found. It is now on display at the Turks and Caicos National Museum in Grand Turk.

The Bermudians and salt raking

The Turks Islands (Grand Turk and Salt Cay) were occupied by Bermudians of British descent from 1678 onwards. The Bermudians came on a seasonal basis to rake and gather the salt that formed in the Islands' lagoons. Gradually, these naturally occurring **salinas** were reinforced to enhance the natural evaporation process, and a system of sluices powered by windmills was installed to control the flow of water.

The hardships endured by the early salt rakers were described in the *Gentleman's Magazine* of 1764:

The business of salt raking is chiefly carried on by Bermudians who come here in the month of March and continue during the dry season, leading a life which the idea of liberty only can render preferable to slavery itself. They live in little huts ... they have a knife in their pockets and a check shirt and a pair of trousers; their food is salt pork, or now and then an iguana when they have the time to catch them, and very often they are without bread. Yet, in this way of life they enjoy health, nor do they ever differ about property or religion, for they have neither priest, lawyer or physician among them.

A view across Grand Turk's salinas (ALAN WIZEMANN)

At first the Bermudians collected salt for their own use but gradually the commodity became an important source of trade and indeed the backbone of the Bermudian economy for well over 100 years. The Bermudians established permanent settlements on Grand Turk, Salt Cay and South Caicos. Bermudian names such as Smith, Lightbourne and Taylor are still common in the Turks Islands today.

In the eighteenth century, the Turks Islands were occupied briefly by France in 1753. Later, the Turks Islands, still settled by Bermudians, became increasingly under the influence of the Bahamas and there were acrimonious exchanges between the settlers who wished to be free of Bahamian control - and taxes - and the House of Assembly in Nassau.

The British government disregarded the settlers' protests and, in 1764, it was adjudged that the Turks and Caicos Islands were part of the Bahamas. Accordingly, in 1767, the Governor of the Bahamas, William Shirley, appointed an agent, Andrew Symmer, to represent him in Grand Turk. In a letter written shortly after his appointment, Symmer described the salt industry and Grand Turk as it seemed to him in 1767:

... The salt on these Islands is deemed equal, if not superior, to any in the world for curing fish and salting meat. The quantity made is considerable and may amount to 300,000 bushels per annum and with good management, it may be augmented to one third more. But since my arrival I have employed myself principally in examining the soil and find it very proper for raising of cotton. The settlers are busy in laying out cotton plantations, and I am hopeful in 18 months to send cotton of our raising to Great Britain.

... In order to make regulations for maintaining tranquillity and order till such time as His Majesty's pleasure should be further known, I have likewise at the earnest request of the inhabitants, given public notice that on 1st May, I shall attend in order to lay out in equal divisions the Salt Ponds on these Islands, reserving the entire property of the ponds to His Majesty and giving the settlers liberty to work the several divisions on paying of His Majesty, his heirs and successors one half penny Sterling per bushel which I hope will be sufficient to defray all the civil expenses of this government.

... The Islands called the Caicos which lie about two leagues to the Westward are from every advice I can learn, of the greatest consequence and I have the strongest reasons to believe (Jamaica excepted) the finest Islands belonging to His Majesty. The lands are level, well watered, rich and capable of producing sugar, indigo and every commodity in common with the other West Indian islands.

There are a number of vessels belonging to these Islands who make it their principal business to go in search of wrecks, a tenth part by way of duty belongs to His Majesty. ... I reckon, in four weeks' time, the number of male settlers here will amount to upwards of 500 white men and if His Majesty shall think proper to give me his orders to settle the Caicos, I am certain that the sum which may be raised by the sale of lands, will bring a sum of money to His Majesty's Treasury, equal to the ceded lands by the Peace.

In March, Symmer wrote to the Governor again:

I have since my arrival laid out two towns in lots, which are taken up by settlers as fast as they can be run out, and have likewise allocated to every family 12 acres of ground for planting cotton and raising provisions.

The situation of Turks Islands with regards Puerto Rico, Hispaniola and Cuba makes it the fittest place for a medium of trade between Great Britain, her American colonies and the French and Spanish inhabitants of the above opulent islands, that is to be found in the West Indies.

… The Bay where the vessels for the convenience of taking salt, usually ride, is on the West side of the Island. In the winter season, there are at times northwest winds in which case, vessels anchor at a place called Hawk's Nest, which is a safe bay and where 500 sail may safely ride.

I have taken particular care to reserve on this and Salt Kay, all the ponds for His Majesty and the pains which will be taken this year to cleanse and improve them, will render them a valuable mine for our fisheries in North America.

Despite the enthusiastic tone in Symmer's letters to his boss, the Bermudian settlers became very disgruntled at Bahamian attempts to control and tax their affairs. In 1769, Symmer wrote to the Governor:

The settlers here are alarmed to the greatest degree for fear they must be subject to the Legislative authority of Providence (Nassau), in which case they are unanimously determined to leave the Island.

By this time, allegations of corruption and involvement in smuggling were being made against Symmer and in 1770, Governor Shirley wrote to the Secretary of State for the Colonies, the Earl of Hillsborough:

I find the steps that I have undertaken in order to put a stop to the unbounded illicit trade which has been carried on in the Turks Islands under the cloak of the salt trade, has caused a great deal of murmuring among the traders who have frequented the place ever since Mr Symmer's arrival there, and do at present in some degree hurt the real salt rakers.

The lengthy protests to London were in vain though, because in 1799 the Turks and Caicos were federated with the Bahamas.

The correspondence between Andrew Symmer and the Governor of the Bahamas, as well as other documents relating to the Turks and Caicos Islands, are at the Public Records Office, Kew, England, in the Colonial Office (CO) collection.

The French invasion
In 1783, just before the end of the American War of Independence, a French force seized the Turks Islands and successfully fought off an

attack by the Captain of HMS *Albemarle*, the young Horatio Nelson. The British regained control soon afterwards.

The Loyalist settlement

The Loyalists were Americans who had fought for the British during the American War of Independence and were afterwards banished from their native land. Some of the Loyalist planters who arrived in Nassau with their slaves in the 1780s were granted land in the then uninhabited Caicos Islands.

Research carried out by Dr Charlene Kozy, published in 1983 in her paper *A History of the Georgia Loyalists and the Plantation Period in the Turks and Caicos Islands*, has established that 72 Loyalists were granted a total of 18 138 acres in the Caicos Islands between 1789 and 1791. Appraisals and conveyances show that more than 80 plantations were established and a missionary's report of 1790 states that the Caicos had 900 inhabitants.

The Loyalists did not stay long, however, as the Islands were found to be ill-suited for growing cotton and sugar. The plantations survived for 30 years before soil exhaustion, unsuitable land, weevils and hurricanes

The Anglican Church on South Caicos was built by the Bermudian settlers

led to their being abandoned. Some of the planters died in the Islands and were buried there, others moved to Grand Turk and entered the salt trade, but the majority went to other parts of the West Indies, Canada or Britain.

The Loyalists left behind few written records, and today their only material legacies are the ruined walls and broken fences of their abandoned plantations. It is known that the village of Lorimers on Middle Caicos was named after Dr Lorimers, a Loyalist who settled close by, and Whitby on North Caicos may well have been named after the English home town of another Loyalist, Thomas Brown. James Misick, a young planter who was granted lands on North Caicos, is known to have enlisted in the Royal Navy in the Anglo-American War of 1812 when he was captured by the Americans. On his release, he became a leading member of the Turks Islands' Legislature and acted as Administrator on several occasions.

When the Loyalists left, their slaves and their descendants were abandoned to survive as best they could from subsistence farming and fishing. Examples of Loyalist surnames are Hall, Robinson, Gardiner and Williams.

The split with Nassau

As pointed out by Michael Craton in his *History of the Bahamas*, published in 1968, Bahamian rule was never either popular or efficient in the Turks and Caicos Islands:

Although the Salt tax had produced, between 1827 and 1847, a quarter of the revenue of the Bahamas, it was clear that less than half the money benefited the Turks Islands in any way. And, although the price of salt had fallen to 3 1/2d per bushel in 1845, the same tax was collected as when the price stood at 1s 3d a bushel.

The orders regulating the salt ponds were detested in the Turks Islands. The Islands were represented in the House of Assembly in Nassau, but owing to the distance they had to travel, the members rarely sat, and when they did, they felt like aliens in an unfriendly land.

The only Bahamians the Turks ever saw were tax collectors. The mail boat from Nassau went to Long Cay once a month but it only went to Grand Turk four times a year. Boats going to England and Jamaica, however, stopped there and the Islanders felt more akin to Kingston than Nassau.

After continual complaints to the British government by the Islanders, the Governor of the Bahamas finally carried out an investigation into their complaints as a result of which a separation was recommended.

In 1848, the Islands were granted a separate charter providing for internal self-government under a Presidency. Captain Frederick Fort was appointed as the first president, administering the Islands' affairs through a Legislative Board which was elected by those taxpayers who were able to read and write. This internal self-rule was subject to the superintendence of the Governor of Jamaica.

The 1866 hurricane

The Presidency started off propitiously. The new system seemed to be working well and the salt economy was prosperous. This happy state of affairs was swept away in a few hours, however, by one of the worst hurricanes ever experienced in the Turks and Caicos and the Bahamas.

The hurricane hit Grand Turk in the evening of 30 September 1866 and by the next day, the country was ruined. Overall, it caused 63 deaths and destroyed more than 750 homes. More than a million bushels of salt were washed away in the tidal wave that followed. The salt markets became depressed in the following years and in 1872 the Islanders 'beseeched' Queen Victoria to annex the Turks and Caicos to Jamaica.

1873–1976

Jamaican rule turned out to be no more popular in the Turks and Caicos than Bahamian rule before it. The Islands derived little or no benefit from the growing economic strength of the Jamaican economy and they fell into relative obscurity.

To a large extent, the Islanders continued to run their own affairs through a Legislative Board under a Commissioner. Eventually, when Jamaica became independent in 1962, the Islands became a separate dependency. However, it was only when the Bahamas became independent in 1962 that the Turks and Caicos acquired their own Governor.

One of Salt Cay's windmills (*opposite*) (TURKS AND CAICOS ISLANDS TOURIST BOARD)

1976

In 1976, following widespread demand, the Turks and Caicos Islands were granted a new Constitution, which established an elected Ministerial form of government under a Chief Minister. The first Chief Minister, JAGS McCartney, who enjoyed a charismatic following, was killed in an air crash in the United States in 1979. His party, The People's Democratic Movement (PDM) contested the election that followed on an independence ticket and was defeated by Norman Saunders' Progressive National Party (PNP) which opposed independence.

In 1985, Mr Saunders and two of his colleagues were arrested in the United States. Subsequently, a Commission of Inquiry was held on Grand Turk, as a result of which the PNP government was forced to resign in July 1986 and the Constitution was amended to allow the Governor to administer the territory through a nominated Advisory Council for an interim period.

Elections were not held until March 1988, when the PDM won a majority at the polls under its leader, Oswald Skippings, who became Chief Minister. In 1991, the PDM was defeated at the polls and C Washington Misick became Chief Minister. Four years later, the tables were turned once again and the PDM under Derek Taylor has been in power since.

The economy

Economically, the Turks and Caicos Islands have had to adjust to the demise of the salt industry in 1964 and to the closure of the two US bases on Grand Turk, each of which led to a great loss of jobs and revenue. Tourism is now the mainstay of the economy although fishing and the processing and exporting of conch and lobster are also of importance.

The offshore finance sector is also of increasing importance to the economy and has been given a major boost by the formation of an Offshore Finance Unit and the introduction of new legislation, including amendments to the Companies Ordinance as well as new Insurance, Banking and Trusts legislation.

The developing Turtle Cove as seen from the air *(previous pages)*
(ANTHONY TAYLOR)

The main focus of the economy is now centred on Providenciales. 'Provo' as it is known for short, was an isolated, sparsely populated island with no air strip until it was 'discovered' by a group of wealthy Americans in the 1960s. Enchanted with the Island and what they saw as its potential, they struck a deal with the British government whereby they would buy and develop a large section of it, in return for the provision of basic infrastructure.

Today, Provo is a cosmopolitan community consisting of Turks and Caicos Islanders and foreign residents from all over the world. Economic growth outstripped the North American economies by about ten per cent in 2000. It is considered the fastest growing economy in the Caribbean, with real estate prices doubling in the last few years. People from elsewhere in the Turks and Caicos have come to live on Provo in search of better opportunities and higher salaries and some of the wealthiest business people include Islanders.

| 4 |
Grand Turk

The capital of the Turks and Caicos Islands, Grand Turk, is also one of the smallest of the inhabited islands at just 7 miles long and 1.5 miles wide, and lies with its length on a north-south axis. Cockburn Town is the name of the settlement, while Grand Turk is the name of the Island itself, though the latter is the only name that is ever used.

Owing to the Island's lack of size it is quite easy to get around, mostly on foot if you have the time, although a short taxi ride is needed to get from one end to the other. Car and scooter hire is also available. The main point of interest is **Front Street**, which runs north-south and is on the west side of the Island at the sea's edge. This narrow but paved street is home to a wide range of buildings, homes, dive shops and hotels and restaurants. Two of the best places to stay and eat are the **Salt Raker Inn** at the southern end and, a few yards north of

The shaded and picturesque Front Street on Grand Turk (ALAN WIZEMANN)

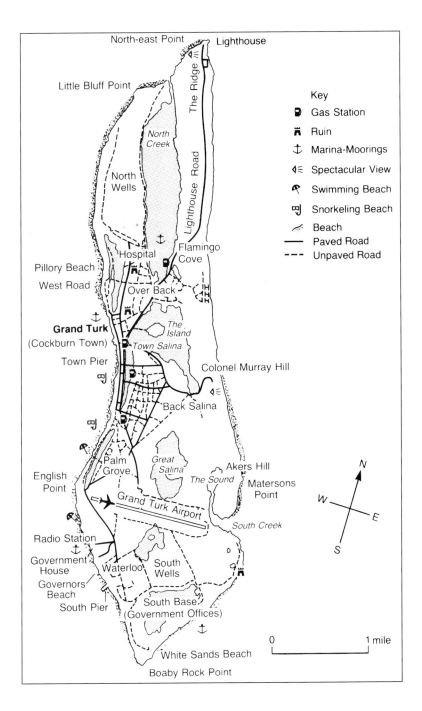

North-east Point   Lighthouse

Little Bluff Point

The Ridge

North Creek

Lighthouse Road

North Wells

Key

🅱 Gas Station

⚓ Ruin

⚓ Marina-Moorings

◀ Spectacular View

☂ Swimming Beach

☂ Snorkeling Beach

〜 Beach

— Paved Road

--- Unpaved Road

Flamingo Cove

Hospital

Pillory Beach

West Road

Over Back

Grand Turk
(Cockburn Town)

The Island

Town Salina

Town Pier

Colonel Murray Hill

Back Salina

Palm Grove

Great Salina

Akers Hill

English Point

The Sound

Matersons Point

Grand Turk Airport

South Creek

Radio Station

Government House

Waterloo

South Wells

Governors Beach

South Pier

South Base
(Government Offices)

White Sands Beach

Boaby Rock Point

N
W   E
S

0   1 mile

Grand Turk

33

The popular Salt Raker Inn (ALAN WIZEMANN)

The Turk's Head Inn is a great place for lunch or dinner (ALAN WIZEMANN)

One of Grand Turk's many beautiful buildings (ALAN WIZEMANN)

The new sea wall on Front Street (ALAN WIZEMANN)

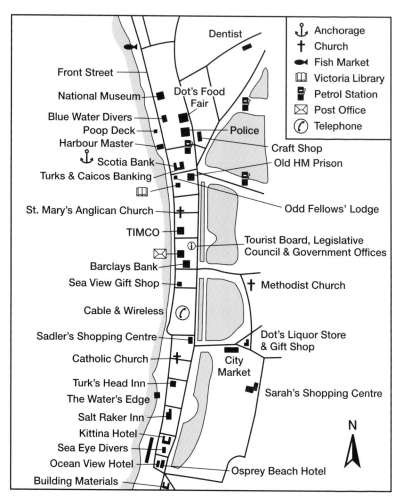

Downtown Grand Turk

that, the **Turk's Head Inn**. Built in the 1840s, this building has been many things including a home, the US Consulate and a doctor's surgery. Its beautiful shaded courtyard is an ideal place to stop for refreshments.

Front Street's attractions don't stop there, though. A few yards further on the **Post Office** and the **Legislative Council** offices come into view. Guarded by canons believed to have come from the ship HMS *Endymion*, and with striking West Indian architecture, they are an impressive sight. Also on Front Street is the **Victoria Public Library**, the old **HM Prison** and **Odd Fellows' Lodge**, from which it is

The historic Eunice Lodge, one of Grand Turk's masonic lodges (ALAN WIZEMANN)

The Turks and Caicos National Museum is one
of the country's great treasures (ALAN WIZEMANN)

believed the proclamation abolishing slavery in the Islands was read in 1832. Perhaps the best known and most visited building is at the top end of the street and is called Guinep House, home of the **Turks and Caicos National Museum.** There is much to see at the museum with artifacts from the New World's oldest shipwreck, the **Molasses Reef Wreck,** the once world famous salt industry and the Island's first settlers, the Arawak Indians. The Molasses wreck was armed with state-of-the-art weapons for the time, and some of these can been seen on display. Only ten years ago the building was little more than a shell but extensive renovations have seen it transformed into a suitably charming home for the nation's heritage. Since its creation in 1991, the Museum has been collecting and safeguarding objects, conducting historical research, advising the government and coordinating the work of visiting researchers. There is also a small shop selling locally-made crafts and a selection of Caribbean books.

However, there is more to Grand Turk than just Front Street. One of the other more prominent points of interest is the Governor's residence, **Waterloo.** The name was given to the building after it was built in 1815, the year of the famous Battle of Waterloo. The residence is situated at the southern end of the Island, next to Governor's beach. It is now home to Grand Turk's first ever golf course. The nine-hole course was built by recent Governor Kelly. Waterloo and its golf course is not open to the public except by special invitation. Also of note is perhaps the world's most travelled lighthouse. Built in Victorian times in London the **Lighthouse** was shipped to the Islands in 1852 and is situated at the northern end of the Island. It is worth noting that you will need a car to get there. Take the Lighthouse Road until you get to the abandoned US base; once here take the dirt road to the left of the perimeter fence until you reach the lighthouse.

Beaches

While Grand Turk may not be blessed with a beach as stunning, or as big, as Provo's Grace Bay beach, there are several to choose from. The best swimming beaches are at Pillory Beach, in front of the old **Guanahani Beach Hotel**, Governor's Beach and the beach directly in front of the Salt Raker Inn. Beware of the heat as Governor's Beach is the only one that offers shade.

Straw dolls, baskets and hats are made by Island women *(opposite)*

An old stone boat slipway leads to the Island's crystal clear waters (ALAN WIZEMANN)

Young members of the Girls' Brigade chatting on Front Street, Grand Turk
(TURKS AND CAICOS ISLANDS TOURIST BOARD)

Things to do

Grand Turk is not about bustling nightlife and entertainment. While there are bars and restaurants open in the evenings, the Island is a quiet place, with most visitors seeking either a secluded island getaway and solitude, or the diving. However, there are several good places to eat and drink, a selection of which follows.

Restaurants

Arawak Inn Restaurant and Bar (Tel: 946 2277)
This serves local and American food, with daily 'specials' including fresh lobster and grouper. It's a great place for sunsets as the bar overlooks the ocean and pristine beach.

Calico Jacks at the Turk's Head Inn (Tel: 946 2466)
Located on Front Street it is open for breakfast, lunch and dinner and serves a variety of cuisine. Dining is either indoors, in the garden terrace or upstairs on the deck, which provides excellent ocean views.

The Sea Eye dive shack (ALAN WIZEMANN)

Jan and Dave's Conch Café at Water's Edge (Tel: 946 1680)
Also on Front Street, this popular café serves conch in a multitude of
ways as well as hamburgers, grouper sandwiches, steak and lobster.

Secret Garden Restaurant at the Salt Raker Inn (Tel: 946 2260)
This is an excellent place to eat offering an array of dishes including
pasta, steaks and the ubiquitous lobster. The *Secret Garden* is also popular on Wednesday nights when the 'rock star that never was', Mitch
Rollings plays live music.

The Courtyard Café at the Osprey Beach Hotel (Tel: 946 2260)
At the southern end of Front Street, the café is open for breakfast,
lunch and dinner, in the charming ambience of its shaded courtyard.

Salt Cay

There are few, if any, places in the world that can quite prepare you for
a first visit to Salt Cay. This tiny island, nestled in the southeast corner
of the Turks and Caicos, just below Grand Turk, was once a thriving
metropolis compared to today. In the early part of the last century it
was one of the world's finest salt producing locations and home to
over 1100 people. Then the bottom dropped out of the industry in the
1960s and people left in droves, virtually abandoning the Island and
a whole way of life. All that was left were the salinas, windmills and
the other signs of a once booming industry, exposed to the merciless
effects of heat and salt. It remained that way until now when, thanks to
the ease and vogue of global travel, it is arguably one of the finest,
secluded island retreats. It also is the permanent home to 65 people
plus a few cows, donkeys and dogs.

The streets of Salt Cay are neat and tidy, although not really paved,
and are often bordered by well-kept walled gardens. The Island is domi-
nated by the now abandoned salinas and by the **White House**, the
home of one of the Bermudian families who used to run the salt industry on the Island. In 1940 Paramount Pictures made a film entitled
Bahama Passage starring Madelaine Carroll, Sterling Haydon and Flora
Robson, which was filmed on location in Salt Cay, in the White House
and also in the recently renovated three-bedroom guest house, **Salt
Cay Sunset House** (formerly the Brown House). The film was based on
the book, *Dildo Cay*, written by Nelson Hayes and published in 1940.

Sunset from the Water's Edge restaurant *(preceding pages)* (ALAN WIZEMANN)

One of Salt Cay's pretty gardens

The White House is still owned by the same family that owned it in the days of the salt industry. Today it is looked after by Mr Lionel Talbot, who is highly knowledgeable about the house and the Island.

Another prominent family on Salt Cay was the Morgan family and for many years the late James Morgan's guest house was one of the few places on Salt Cay where visitors could stay. Today Mr Morgan's guest house, re-named **Mount Pleasant Guest House** has new owners, American Bryan Sheedy and his wife. Although Mr Sheedy recently moved to Grand Turk, his guest house is still open and in the good care of Salt Cay native, Nathan Smith. Nathan is Salt Cay's own entrepreneur and as well as guest house manager, wears the hats of taxi driver, golf cart rental operator and airline ticket agent to name a few. If you need it, Nathan is your man.

Salt Cay's treasures aren't all on land, however. The wreck of the HMS *Endymion* lies in 25 feet of water in a lovely coral canyon teeming with all kinds of marine life. The *Endymion* sank in 1790 while carrying 560 men, 40 canons and four 15-foot anchors.

Perhaps even more remarkable is the exquisite white marble cenotaph of one Jane Jones, which lies in 20 feet of water just behind the White House. Carving on the tomb, crafted in New York, tells us that Jane died in November 1813 'in the 21st year of her age'. While we

can't be certain how she died, many believe it was the hurricane which hit the Island at that time which took her life.

At the east end of the Island, there is the quaint, eight-room **Windmills** hotel, which was designed and built over a period of ten years by its owner - architect Mr Guy Lovelace. Located on a two-mile beach, the hotel, designed in a predominantly Bermudian style, offers accommodation to those who want to 'get away from it all'. It has recently been leased by Jim and Sharon Shafer, long term operators of Pine Cay. There are also several other guest houses and restaurants on Salt Cay as well as dive operators. Further information can be found in Chapter 8 towards the back of this book.

The Cays

It is possible to take a boat to visit some of the outlying uninhabited cays, such as **Round**, **Gibbs** and **East Cay**, which support a variety of plant and bird life.

The beach at Gibb's Cay (*preceding pages*)

| 5 |
Providenciales

One of the most isolated of the Caicos Islands until the 1960s, Providenciales is now the centre of development in the country. It is believed the Island was named by survivors of a shipwrecked French boat called *La Providentielle* who were washed up here. At 14 miles long and several miles wide, you will need a car to get around. Like all the Caicos Islands, 'Provo' has a much higher rainfall than Grand Turk, which means that it is much greener all year round.

It is only since the 1980s that development has spread further than the first three original fishing villages of **Blue Hills**, **Five Cays** and **The Bight**. These still remain though the rest of the Island has changed dramatically with most of the development concentrated between Downtown and the eastern, Leeward, end of the Island. Great areas of the western end of the island are designated Crown Land and are, as yet, untouched by development.

The last few years have seen the greatest rate of development in terms of hotels, resorts, restaurants and tourist arrivals. To cope with the growth in tourism a new multi-million dollar airport was opened in 1999. This is a constant hive of activity with over 40 international flights arriving weekly as well as the numerous inter-island flights by the four locally owned carriers. The airport is also home to **Gilley's Café**. Gilley's serves as a popular place to meet and eat for many residents as well as an ideal place to pass the time for departing tourists. It is open from 6 am until 8 pm and serves breakfast, lunch and dinner in a comfortable air-conditioned setting.

Downtown

This is something of a misnomer as many people expect a thriving, bustling commercial and residential area. It has only been in existence for around 15 years and consists of shops and offices around **Butterfield Square**. Art Butterfield, the developer, was originally from North Caicos, and is one of the pioneers behind Provo's development. The **Town Centre Mall** is the main building in the square and while it houses one of two supermarkets on the Island, it is largely made up of

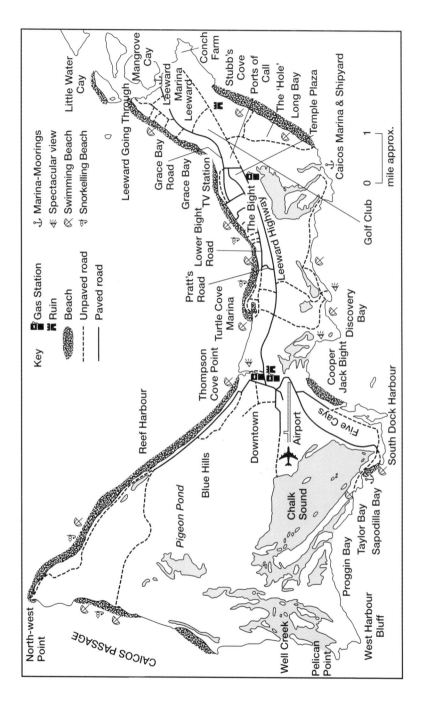

Providenciales

offices for law firms, a utility company, bank and a travel agent to name a few. There are no retail shops as one might have expected.

Across the road there is another square and again this houses a bank and various offices, although nestled in the corner is **Tasty Temptations** delicatessen. This is a residents' favourite for breakfast and lunch as proprietor, Denis Levesque, bakes his own breads, pastries and muffins freshly every morning. There are also various government offices located here as well as the American Airlines service centre.

Chalk Sound

Most of Provo's development has been to the east of Downtown, which itself happens to be geographically fairly central on the Island. However, if you arrived by air during daylight hours you will have flown over **Chalk Sound** and might have noticed its striking turquoise water. This is caused by its shallow depth (around 20 feet) and heavily silted bottom. The road to Chalk Sound is undulating and paved, with several blind bends and entrances, so caution is urged when driving, especially at night. At the end of this road is **South Dock** which is

Coconut palms fringe the seaside village of Blue Hills

Provo's deep-water freight dock. To the right of this, and just after the turning to Chalk Sound, is a small hill with a path to the top. Not only does the brief walk to the summit afford excellent views over the area, there are several rock carvings from ship-wrecked sailors. Replica casts of these hang in the departure area at the airport.

The long spit of land which separates the Sound from the ocean has unsurprisingly been a magnet for privates homes and villas, some of which are available for holiday rental. There are two superb beaches here, **Sapodilla Bay** beach and **Taylor Bay** beach. Both are excellent for swimming and are never over-populated even in high season. The Sound is a national park and no motorised vessels are allowed inside, although kayaking and windsurfing are allowed.

Turtle Cove

This was the first area developed, in the 1960s, by the group of wealthy Americans known locally as *The Seven Dwarfs*, which included at least one Roosevelt and a Dupont. The turn-off from Leeward Highway down to Turtle Cove is called **Suzie Turn** and was named after a secretary called Suzie working in the Cove who could never remember where the turning was. Her friends put up a sign saying 'Suzie, turn!'. Suzie and the original sign have long gone but the name has stuck and a new sign stands proudly. The first complex to be built at **Turtle Cove** was the, now dilapidated, **Third Turtle Inn**. The Inn may have closed but the area has become a focal point with an excellent new marina, shops, restaurants, and apartments. It also plays host to the two billfish tournaments held on Provo each year. The beach is only a few minutes walk and is accessible by the dirt road past the **Sharkbite**. It offers one of the two best snorkelling sites on Provo, called **Smith's Reef**.

If you come into the marina by boat you may be able to see one of the resident pair of ospreys in the nest on the left bank. These stunning and large birds of prey are a rare sight in many areas of the world, but have been left untouched here in the Islands. They can often be seen eating their latest catch, perched upon one of the many large timber mooring poles in the marina.

A stunning view over the Cove and out into Grace Bay can be seen from the **Mirimar Resort**, previously known as the **Erebus Inn**, and its restaurant, which occupy a commanding position on the hill over the Cove. There is also a fully equipped gym and physiotherapy centre, as well as a pool and tennis courts on-site.

Grace Bay Club, Providenciales

The Bight

The road out from Turtle Cove heading east toward **Grace Bay** is called the **Lower Bight Road** and is somewhat less busy than **Leeward Highway**, which runs parallel to it down the middle of the Island. They join together at the **Ports of Call** and **Allegro Resort** junction and from there they become the only road out further east toward **Leeward**. Taking this road from Turtle Cove you pass through The Bight. This area is striking not for its beauty, but for the fact that it highlights the disparity between the multi-million dollar resorts such as **Beaches**, **The Alexandria** and **The Sands**, which line its beach side in that order, and the relative poverty in which many Turks Island natives and the immigrant Haitian population live.

There is access to the beach at various points with a favourite being beside the clearly sign-posted, **Coral Gardens** condominium resort. Known as the **Whitehouse Reef**, this is the second prime snorkelling spot. As with Smith's Reef, there is a snorkel-trail which is worth following. Neither site has shade, and there is nowhere to buy refreshments, so make sure you bring both if you plan to spend any time there.

The vast Beaches resort on Grace Bay *(overleaf)* (ANTHONY TAYLOR)

A new environmental visitor centre is under construction at the corner of the Lower Bight Road and **Pratt's Road**. The latter road heads up a hill going south and rejoins Leeward Highway just west of the Island's major supermarket, the **IGA**. Opposite this new centre is a community park, right on the beach, which boasts a children's climbing frame. There is also a small graveyard, on the ocean side, whose bright, white and well-tended tombstones catch the eye.

Grace Bay: Ports of Call to Leeward

Ports of Call is the Island's best area for shopping. A new development, it boasts a large hotel in the Comfort Suites group, and a two-storey complex which is home to three restaurants, an Internet café, car rental operator, **Dive Provo** dive shop, gym, architects, **Remax** realty and a variety of clothing and gift stores.

Just a little further along the road is the smaller **Grace Bay Plaza**, which is home to the excellent **Caicos Café** restaurant, **Caicos Adventures** dive shop, a hairstylists and several other clothing, craft and gift stores. This part of Grace Bay has seen the most development with resorts such as **Royal West Indies, Ocean Club West** (sister to the older **Ocean Club**) and The Sands, joining the Island's established resorts, **Grace Bay Club** and Club Med. Each of these have excellent restaurants attached to them, serving a combination of breakfast, lunch and dinner. More current information on these can be found in one of the several tourist magazines available. All of these are on the now world famous **Grace Bay Beach**, listed by *Condé Naste Traveller* magazine as one of the top five beaches anywhere in the world. One point worth noting is that, unlike many other destinations, there are no private beaches in the Turks and Caicos, which means access to the beach is available at numerous locations, although some resorts may object to non-guests using sun-loungers.

Should you fancy a slightly more active stay, then one of the Caribbean's finest golf courses can be found just over a mile from Ports of Call. **Provo Golf Club**, which was designed by Karl Litton, is a challenging 18-hole course; it played host in 1999 to the Caribbean Open Championship. Its beautiful clubhouse is home to the excellent **Fairways Bar and Grill** which serves breakfast, lunch and dinner and is open to non-playing guests.

The Islands are best known for their pristine, calm waters and world class diving. **Leeward Marina** is the home to many of the Islands'

The clubhouse at Provo Golf Club, from the eighteenth green (ALAN WIZEMANN)

operators including **Big Blue**, **J and B Tours** and **Silver Deep** to name three. It can be found at the end of **Grace Bay Road** in the Leeward development, which is still partly owned by the millionaire owner of Belize Bank, Mr Michael Ashcroft. There are the usual marina facilities including a large fishing store. JoJo the wild and world famous dolphin can often be spotted all along Grace Bay from the shore including at the marina, where he playfully follows the boats.

No visit to Leeward or Provo would be complete without a tour of the **Conch Farm** at the eastern-most tip of Leeward. To get there take the Leeward road straight on instead of bearing left to the marina. The **Ashcroft School**, named after its benefactor Michael Ashcroft, with its white building and green trim, is on your right and the road shortly after this becomes a wide dirt road and leads to the farm. This is the first and only commercial conch farm in the world.

On leaving the conch farm, if you follow the road straight and don't turn right back to Leeward, it goes for about two miles before rejoining the paved Leeward Highway at **Temple Plaza**, half a mile south of Ports of Call. Halfway along this road is the entrance to the **Long Bay** area. Largely undeveloped, it has a superb three-mile beach which is a beachcomber's paradise.

Leeward's calm waters are ideal for kayak eco-tours (ANTHONY TAYLOR)

One of Leeward's many stunning homes (ANTHONY TAYLOR)

Things to do

As might be expected, Provo is geared more toward tourists than are the other Islands and as a result there is considerably more to do. Water sports feature greatly, and there are numerous dive sites and cays to explore and plenty of operators to take you. While none of the Islands have the nightlife of other Caribbean countries, there are several places you can go to eat, drink and dance into the small hours. **Latitudes**, on a Friday night at Ports of Call, is a favourite, as is the recently opened and dedicated nightclub, **Stardust and Ashes** on Leeward Highway just before Temple Plaza. There are several excellent bands on Provo and they play at several locations. There are also many sporting opportunities including tennis, squash, parasailing and deep-sea sport fishing.

More sedate options include a visit to the 'Hole', a collapsed limestone sink hole in **Long Bay** on **Seasage Hill Drive**. At 40 feet across and some 80 feet deep it's quite a sight, though there are no railings so care and a close watch on children is required. The remains of one of the early Loyalist plantations, **Cheshire Hall**, are located opposite **Royal Jewels'** Downtown store and next to the **Myrtle Rigby Health Clinic**.

Eating out is easy, although with over 40 different establishments to choose from, selecting one might not be. The list is too extensive to detail here but excellent guides can be found in publications such as *Times of the Islands* and on the Internet, for example at the **TCI Search** web-site (see Chapter 8).

The Cays

Between Providenciales and North Caicos lie a number of Cays. Iguanas are the only inhabitants of **Little Water Cay**, which is just across from Leeward, to which several operators run daily excursions. **Fort George Cay** was once the home of a British outpost and two canons from the Fort can still be seen in shallow water at the site. Further along is **Pine Cay**, named after the Cuban pine that thrives on the edges of its freshwater ponds. Pine Cay is home to the **Meridian Club**, an exclusive private resort.

The last island before North Caicos is **Parrot Cay**, which is in fact a corruption of *Pirate* Cay. In the eighteenth century the Turks and Caicos were a haven for all manner of pirates and Pirate Cay was known to be the haunt of one famous pirate called 'Calico' Jack Rackam, so called for his penchant for wearing cotton clothing. Rackam was accompanied by two female pirates, Mary Reid and Anne Bonny,

who, when they came to trial in Jamaica, were described by one witness as follows:

> *The two women on Rackam's sloop wore men's jackets and long trousers and handkerchiefs tied about their heads, and that each of them had a pistol in their hands ... They were both very profligate, cursing and swearing and willing to do anything on board.*

Rackam was eventually hanged in Jamaica. The two women, both of whom were pregnant, were sentenced to imprisonment. Mary Reid died of fever in prison, but Anne Bonny won a reprieve, and spent the rest of her life in Virginia, married to a doctor she had freed from capture during a pirating venture.

Today, Parrot Cay is more famous for its high class resort which plays host to many movies stars such as Bruce Willis, and ex-Beatle, Sir Paul McCartney.

The friendly nurse shark is a common sight among the shallow water reefs of the country *(opposite)* (PHIL SHEARER)

| 6 |
The Caicos Islands

North Caicos

In contrast to Providenciales, the neighbouring island of North Caicos is very rural with three isolated settlements. Until 30 years ago, the Islanders lived from subsistence farming. Since then, the arrival of electricity, paved roads, telephones and a few cars, has eased life for the inhabitants of this, one of the Turks and Caicos' most beautiful islands. Until recently, North Caicos rarely attracted much in the way of visitors, now, thanks to a rapidly expanding Provo and more links by air and sea, an increasing number of residents and tourists are making the short trip. Much quieter than Provo, North Caicos boasts better roads, beautiful expanses of beach and lush vegetation and scenery which make cycling tours of the island a must.

A house ruin hints at North Caicos's past history (ALAN WIZEMANN)

The airport and main settlement is at **Bottle Creek**, while the main hotel, the **Prospect of Whitby**, is on the beach at **Whitby**. There are also several other places to stay including the **Pelican Beach Hotel**. The third village, **Kew**, is located inland in the most fertile part of the Island, where gardens abound with vegetables and tropical fruit trees such as custard apples, sapodilla, papaya, mangoes and bananas. It's as a result of this fertility and lushness that many Islanders refer to North Caicos as the 'garden island'.

On the road to Kew is **Cottage Pond**, a large freshwater pond, fringed with primeval-looking vegetation including tree ferns. Also at Kew are the ruins of one of the main loyalist plantations, **Wades Green**. Unsurprisingly, **Flamingo Pond** derives its name from the hundreds of flamingoes which are often sighted there.

There are several methods of travelling to North Caicos, the fastest is a 12-minute flight from Provo, while it is also possible to catch a boat over from Leeward Marina. Local dive operator, Big Blue, also conducts full or half-day tours over to the Island.

A view across Flamingo Pond (ALAN WIZEMANN)

Middle Caicos

The largest of the inhabited islands is Middle Caicos, at 15 miles long and some five miles wide, and it is also the least populated with around 270 people living there. It too has three small settlements, **Conch Bar**, **Lorimers** and **Bambarra**. It is said that Bambarra was given its name by the African survivors of a slave ship which was wrecked off the Island, after the abolition of slavery in the British Empire. Forced to make a new life on the Island, they named their village after their homeland in West Africa. The first settlers, however, were Indians who lived there from 750 AD to around the fourteenth century, and numbered approximately 4000.

The Island is home to an impressive set of caves at Conch Bar as well as some stunning coastal cliffs and scenery, especially at **Mudjin Harbour**. Middle Caicos is also famous for its recently cleared **Crossing Place Trail** - three miles of coastal hiking and biking trails, following the path that early Middle Caicos residents took from Lorimers to cross the sand bars to North Caicos. The beautiful signs were designed and created by resident artists, Pamela Leach and Barbara Young. The popularity of Middle Caicos has increased recently and there are now several places to stay including the beautiful **Blue Horizon Resort**.

Ocean Hole, Middle Caicos

Just offshore of Middle Caicos is **Ocean Hole**, a large, almost perfectly round natural sink hole which plunges thousands of feet from the shallow waters which surround it.

South Caicos

Despite being part of the Caicos Islands, South Caicos, or **The Big South** was one of the centres of the salt industry. It is a more arid island than the other Caicos Islands though not as dry as Grand Turk.

Conch and lobster fishing are the main industries on South Caicos and there are processing and freezing plants at the port in **Cockburn Harbour**. Like Grand Turk and Salt Cay, Cockburn Harbour features many stone-walled streets and Bermudian and West Indian style architecture.

The Big South is also home to one of the Islands' longest and most popular festivals, the **South Caicos Regatta**. This annual event takes place at the end of May and is one of the most colourful of the

Children enjoying the South Caicos Regatta

65

Maypole dancing at the South Caicos Regatta

annual festivals, with music and dancing taking over from boat racing during the evening.

East and West Caicos

Both of these Islands are uninhabited and are Crown Land. The remains of a Loyalist plantation can still be seen at **Jacksonville** on East Caicos. On West Caicos, **Lake Catherine** is an important gathering point for many species of migratory birds and for flamingoes, while just offshore are numerous dive sites to which several Provo based operators make weekly visits.

| 7 |
Island dishes

You can't be in the Turks and Caicos for long without realising the important part played in the country's life and culture by the beautiful tropical shellfish, the Queen Conch (*Strombus gigas*). Seafood, conch in particular, has always been an important item in the diet of most islanders.

Wild conch live in the turtle grass found in shallow waters surrounding the Islands. They reach maturity at two years and for generations were fished by divers from small boats. Conch features widely on the menus of virtually every restaurant in the country in a variety of forms: conch fritters, cracked conch, conch stew, conch salad and conch chowder.

Its importance to the life and economy of the country is reflected in the fact that the conch shell is featured on the national flag along with a lobster, the Turk's cap cactus and the flamingo. The Islands are also home to the world's first and only commercial conch farm, located at Leeward. The brainchild of Chuck Hesse the farm has pioneered the rearing and farming of conch since 1985 and now exports to some of the world's most exclusive restaurants. In fact, world famous chef, Alain Ducasse, featured conch from Hesse's farm in his book, *Harvesting Excellence*. It was the only non-US product to be included.

One of the Islands' best exponents of cooking with conch is Simon Poulin, head chef of the **Bay Bistro Restaurant** at the **Sibonne Hotel** on Grace Bay.

| 8 |
Useful information

Getting here

Getting here is now considerably easier than it ever has been, thanks to the increased number of carriers flying into the Islands. There are now around 40 flights a week including scheduled flights via American Airlines out of Miami and Delta Air Lines from Atlanta and a service from the UK with British Airways. On top of that there are numerous charter flights from the US and Canada.

The Islands are also home to four airlines - SkyKing, Turks and Caicos Airways, InterIsland Airways and Global Airways. Of the four, SkyKing and InterIsland are the scheduled operators with the largest fleets of aircraft. Between them there are daily services between many of the local islands and weekly services to the Bahamas, Haiti and the Dominican Republic.

An InterIsland Airways plane waits for its passengers on Salt Cay (ANTHONY TAYLOR)

Immigration

Entry to the Islands is simple. A passport is required, although no visa is needed for citizens of the US and UK, as well as certain other countries, who can stay for a period of 30 days. This can be extended, although you will need to visit the Immigration Department's office in Downtown Provo for approval. All visitors require a return ticket and there is a $20 departure tax. For those wishing to live in the Islands, a resident's permit is needed, while those wishing to work need a work permit. There are strict rules and regulations regarding living and working in the Islands and enquiries should be made to either the Immigration Department (see useful telephone numbers, in this chapter) or to one of the many law firms in the country.

Customs

All persons over the age of 17 may bring with them into the country, duty free: up to one quart of spirits or two litres of wine; 200 cigarettes or 100 cigarillos, or 50 cigars or 125 grams of tobacco; 50 grams of perfume or 0.25 litres of eau de toilette.

In addition, visitors may bring with them, as gifts, dutiable goods of any other description purchased outside the Islands, to a total value of $200, provided the goods are not prohibited and are not imported for commercial purposes. Firearms and spear-guns are not allowed and must be handed in for safekeeping until departure.

Returning residents are allowed to bring in dutiable goods of up to $200, providing the goods are not prohibited and are not imported for commercial purposes. Persons arriving in the Islands to live and work are allowed to bring in personal effects duty free, providing they intend to remain in the Islands for not less than 12 months.

The duty on imported items is 33 per cent of the purchase price. For more information please contact the Director of Customs.

Health and climate

The Turks and Caicos Islands are a healthy place to live. There are no tropical diseases and no immunisations are required for visitors unless they are coming from an infected area.

The weather in the Islands is warm all year. In the winter, the temperature will sometimes fall to 15°C at night when a blanket may be required. In the summer, most days are hot often reaching past 30°C, though the air is often cooled by the prevailing Trade Winds.

Visitors should be careful to avoid excessive exposure to the sun, which is intense here, and to consume adequate quantities of water. Tap water is safe to drink here too. Visitors should also take the usual precautions with regards to the risk of AIDS and other sexually transmitted diseases. Medical insurance is a must, as while there are several established medical practices on Provo, all are private, and serious injuries and conditions will require evacuation to either the Bahamas or Miami.

Currency
The US dollar is the official currency.

Clothing
Cool, casual clothing is the most suitable for the Islands. Although on Provo beach wear is acceptable in most places, it is not so in town on Grand Turk. There are no restaurants where a tie is required. There are a growing number of shops on Provo where a variety of clothes and shoes can be bought.

Getting around
A car is a necessity on Provo and is recommended over a bike or scooter owing to the poor condition of the roads. There is a major road building scheme planned, but at the time of writing the majority of roads remain unpaved while traffic density is increasing. Please note that the Islands follow the British system and cars drive on the left. However, extra care is due at night as most vehicles are imported from the US and so have their headlights pointing into the face of the oncoming traffic. Drink driving is also a problem and is prevalent at night on the weekends.

There are a number of car rental agencies offering a variety of vehicle types and models. There are also rental operators on the other Islands such as Grand Turk and North Caicos. Hiring a bike or scooter on these Islands is safer as the roads are in better condition with much less traffic.

Neither Providenciales nor Grand Turk have scheduled public transport, however there are a number of taxis available. Standard rates are charged according to distance and the number of passengers, but it is worth agreeing a price before getting in. On North Caicos the two main taxi drivers are Mac Campbell and Tiger; both can be contacted via VHS radio, but their prices are higher than on Provo.

Government and legal framework

The Islands are a **British Overseas Territory**. A Governor, appointed by the UK Foreign Office presides over an Executive Council. The country has its own head of government, the Chief Minister. The Legislative Council is empowered to pass local statutes. The legal framework is based on English Common law and is administered by a Chief Justice and a magistrate.

Telecommunications

All telecommunications services are provided under an agreement with Cable and Wireless, although high-speed Internet access will soon be available through WIV Cable to subscribers. Internet booths are operating at selected outlets on Provo, including the IGA supermarket. There is also an Internet café at Ports of Call shopping centre, opposite the Allegro Resort.

The Royal Turks and Caicos Police Force Band marches past at the Queen's Official Birthday Parade on Grand Turk

71

Media

The local media has grown in recent years and there is now a plethora of information published in the form of newspapers, magazines, radio and guides. There are two newspapers, the *Turks and Caicos Weekly News* and *The Free Press*, and a high quality quarterly magazine called the *Times of the Islands*. There are several tourist-guide publications, the best being *Where When How*. WIV Cable TV provides some 32 channels of television from US feeds as well as locally recorded programmes on Channel 4.

Books and Magazines

The best bookstore in Provo is the **Unicorn Bookshop** run by Linda and Mike St Louis. Here you'll find a wide selection of books, magazines, newspapers and local publications. They are located at The Market Place, P.O. Box 399, Providenciales, Tel: 649 941 5458. Fax: 649 941-5510. Email: unicorn@tciway.tc

Electricity

The electricity supply is 110 volts, 60 cycles, and is suitable for all US appliances.

Festivals and holidays

Several of the festivals and holidays, which are celebrated on the Islands, centre around boating and fishing. There are two regattas, the longest running is the South Caicos Regatta, which was started after a visit of Queen Elizabeth II to the Island on 25 February 1966. This is traditionally held during the weekend nearest to May 24, while the new but extremely popular **Fool's Regatta** is held on Provo during the middle of June.

There are also two major billfish tournaments held every year. The **Classic** is a five-day event held at the start of June, while the **Caicos Cup** is held at the start of July. Both attract large fields ensuring Turtle Cove is awash with beautiful sport fishing boats as well as playing host to a wide range of tournament-long festivities. They are well worth a visit.

A heron on the lookout for a meal in the grounds of the Golf Course
(opposite) (PHIL SHEARER)

The Spanish **Cinque de Mayo** has also caught on in recent years and once again Turtle Cove plays host as all of the dockside restaurants, from the Sharkbite to **Banana Boat**, provide a range of food and beverages to fuel the party which lasts until after midnight.

Real estate

The real estate market in the country has been booming in recent years and there is no sign of a let up with development struggling to keep up with demand. There are opportunities on all the Islands, but the bulk are on Provo and increasingly, North Caicos. There are many realtors in the Islands who can help you to find your ideal home or plot of land. Many of these fall under the umbrella of the **Turks and Caicos Real Estate Association**. It is wise to consult a lawyer or realtor who can explain about stamp duty, land registry and the buying process.

Useful telephone numbers and web-sites

Telephone numbers

The Tourist Board (Provo)	649 946 4970
The Tourist Board (Grand Turk)	649 946 2321
Provo Police (Provo)	649 946 4259
Immigration (Provo)	649 946 4233
American Airlines	649 946 4948
Providenciales Airport	649 941 5670
Menzies Medical Clinic	649 946 4242
Grace Bay Medical Clinic	649 941 5252
Turks and Caicos Real Estate Association	649 946 4602
Scotia Bank	649 946 4750
Barclays Bank	649 946 4245
SkyKing	649 941 5464

Web-sites

Turks and Caicos Real Estate Association	www.tcirealestate.com
Times of the Islands	www.timespub.tc
TCI Search	www.tcisearch.com

Just two of the hundreds of flamingoes that can be seen throughout the Islands *(overleaf)* (PHIL SHEARER)

Bibliography

The Turks and Caicos Islands Beautiful by Nature, by Julia and Phil Davies

Flowers of The Bahamas and Turks and Caicos Islands, by Kathleen McNary Wood

Guides

The Bahamas: Family of Islands, by Gail Saunders

Highly illustrated

Nassau's Historic Landmarks, by Gail Saunders and Linda Huber

The Bahamas Rediscovered, by Nicolas and Dragan Popov

History

The Story of the Bahamas, by Paul Albury

Historic Nassau, by Gail Saunders and Donald Cartwright

Bahamian Loyalists and their Slaves, by Gail Saunders

Natural history

Trees of The Bahamas, by William Cutts

Coral Reefs of the Caribbean, The Bahamas and Florida, by Alfonso Silva Lee and Roger Dooley

The Ephemeral Islands, by David Campbell

Fiction

Oh No! The Pink Flamingo Turned Green, by Marilyn Sheffield

Bahamian Anthology, by The College of The Bahamas

Also available in the
MACMILLAN CARIBBEAN GUIDES SERIES

Anguilla: Tranquil Isle of the Caribbean - Brenda Carty and
    Colville Petty
Antigua and Barbuda: Heart of the Caribbean - Brian Dyde
The Bahamas: Family of Islands - Gail Saunders
Barbados: The Visitors Guide - F A Hoyos
Belize: Ecotourism in Action - Meb Cutlack
The Islands of Bermuda: Another World - David Raine
Dominica: Isle of Adventure - Lennox Honychurch
Grenada: Isle of Spice - Norma Sinclair
Jamaica: The Fairest Isle - Philip Sherlock and Barbara Preston
Nevis: Queen of the Caribees - Joyce Gordon
St Kitts: Cradle of the Caribbean - Brian Dyde
St Lucia: Helen of the West Indies - Guy Ellis
St Vincent and the Grenadines - Lesley Sutty
Tobago: An Introduction and Guide - Eaulin Blondel
USVI: America's Virgin Islands - Arlene Martel